POETRY ANTHOLOGY

AN AGONY OF HOPE

Ananta Dave

ISBN
Paperback 979-8-89277-764-3
Hardcase 979-8-89475-214-3

In loving memory of my mother

Mrs Mylavarapu Janaki

Amma, this is for you -a rare and loving spirit with the spark of creative genius.

CONTENTS

1. A Palette of Light and Shade — 1

2. The Shape of Grief — 3

3. Waiting — 4

4. A Simple Life — 6

5. Pea Soup(Er) — 8

6. The Almost-Pearl in the Moon — 11

7. Tainted and Dented, Expecting to be Treated — 12

8. Until we all Breathe Free Again — 14

9. It is All in the Mind — 16

10. Dare to Dream — 19

11. Lest their Beds Lie Empty Tonight — 22

12. A Place of Safety — 24

13. Wherefore, Stormy Spring? — 27

14. Fire in our Souls — 29

15. The Fragments of a Day — 30

16. A Song of Silence — 31

17. An Inescapable Rightness of Being — 33

18. I Root for Love, one more Time — 35

19. The Voice of Woman — 37

20. No Wrong Door — 38

21. Lest Pride Hold Sway once Again — 40

22. Remnants of the Season   42

23. The Longest Journey   43

24. The Final Touch   47

A PALETTE OF LIGHT AND SHADE

The alleys of my mind

Take a winding route,

Forever trying to catch up

With the real me, the whole of me.

Am I the colour of my skin?

Defined by my birth motherland,

Anointed by my adopted motherland,

Or in no man's land?

Am I like the budding hope of spring,

The unashamed bloom of summer,

Like the mellow crackling of autumn

Or the dreary grey of winter?

Am I the foreigner, the immigrant,

The second-tier citizen, the interloper?

Or a multicultural, able adaptor,

A friend, colleague, key worker, and leader.

Is there space for me, all of me?
Or shall I live my life
As a series of halves,
The segments of an arc, never the full circle?

My meandering thoughts
As always, find refuge in the womb of nature,
Where one tableau flows into another
As frames of a movie coming together.

For the sun is low, then high,
Fiercely bright, then hidden behind clouds,
The moon curves into a sliver, disappears,
And becomes whole again.

My shadow shrinks under the noon sun
And grows tall at the edge of daylight.
Sometimes I whimper and whisper,
At others, burst into glorious song.

I straddle two lands
And the turbulent seas.
These shifting, lifting shades
Are all part of my palette, the whole of me.

THE SHAPE OF GRIEF

Grief was a mountain,

Immovable, impossible to cross,

Looming dark, terrifying,

Casting all in shadow.

Grief was the high tide,

Rushing in relentlessly,

Sweeping all in its wake,

My leaden feet stuck in the sand.

Grief is a sluggish river,

The gentle rhythm broken by small ripples,

The shore across a dull green-brown haze,

The shadows dappled with weak sunshine.

Grief is a dark silhouette in my bed

That shrinks away by day,

Occasionally emerges outside the window

Where pink-hued spring blossoms grow.

WAITING

Waiting for sunrise
And the calls from back home to start.

Dreading the call,
Yearning for the call.
For the neighbour to say,
"Your father is breathing, he is eating."

Waiting for the money transfer to go through.
"You need to pay within two hours or lose the bed."
Parents waiting in Reception for entry into the hospital,
The living and the dead equally silent.

Waiting for air, hell is no oxygen.
"Sorry, ventilator is for four hours only, others are waiting."
"The doctor had a kind voice," my neighbour says
While waiting in the corridor for her beloved's body to be bagged.

Waiting in the car park for the cremation,

His body shrouded in her sari.

Ambulance number 1722, token number 284.

Dozens of pyres lighting the sky, a 42°C summer.

On the long journey home with an empty house waiting.

Waiting at home, imprisoned by the virus.

Waiting for vaccines without borders,

For sharers, not hoarders.

Waiting for larger hearts, smaller egos.

Meanwhile, we live, work, and breathe.

Waiting for the thump-thump of guilt to subside,

For the flood-tide of despair to recede.

Waiting for a different dawn,

Waiting to embrace my motherland and mine.

A SIMPLE LIFE

My mum lives, long after she is gone.
I can feel her gentle lingering,
Emitting shafts of light
That went out quietly a decade ago.

In a dusty, creaking drawer in her room,
A fine-toothed comb, a scrunched hair bun.
Hair clips in black, brown, and silver,
Safety pins nestling with hairpins.

A blue box with needle and thread, hooks, buttons.
Forever mending...
Bright red sticky bindis, a hand mirror,
Handkerchiefs washed and carefully folded.

A few feet away in her wardrobe,
A faint rose fragrance rising through the rusty hinges.
A frayed cardigan I had gifted her years ago,
Light pastel saris neatly folded.

Petticoats and blouses to pair with the saris,

Some cotton nightgowns we had shopped for together.

The few jewels and silk saris

Cleared and distributed by my dad in grim, moist-eyed silence.

The memories frozen in time, preserved in mothballs.

The room untouched by my dad except when we visit.

Mum's delicate features leaping out of a flower-decked photo in the hall,

The efficient kitchen she had designed now meagrely stocked.

Sixty years of a simple life

Rich with dignity and grace.

A soft voice, a ferocious brain

In the memory of a demure gaze, her bright presence lives on.

PEA SOUP(ER)

Migrating to the UK, hey?
Let's help you along the way.
You are a doctor, maybe,
Or have landed on our shores in a dinghy?

Rwanda... racism, did you whisper?
No, it's not a whitewash, nor slander, it's mere banter.
It's to stop those small boats,
It's about people staying alive and afloat.

In any case, don't worry about the colour of your skin,
It's all about inclusion - Black, Brown, or in between.
We can do an induction
Of UK customs and traditions.

So, the alphabet soup, you see,
Is not about a gently floating ABC medley.

You know, the roe is what gives us the lovely caviar.

Oh, don't worry, Roe v Wade was in the US, nothing fishy here.

And pea soup is nice, but pea souper is a fog in any case.

Agree it's not very clear if English is not your first language.

Here, we have a variety of cuisines melding,

From food banks to fine dining.

We do have parties when we want to celebrate,

But do not confuse it with Partygate.*

Yes, there's orderly queuing here; we are a civilised nation.

Child Q** you ask, assure you that case was an aberration.

And the Windrush was a fine ship which fulfilled a requirement.

Let's not hear a word about the hostile environment.

Not everything is to your taste or inclination?

"One man's meat is indeed another man's poison."

Yes, you got that right, I say.

Your English is quite good if I may.

Ok, welcome, and here is the bill for your lodgings.

For the food shop, hope you have some of your savings.

Pay will be at the end of the month,

But do sort out your bank account.

Terms in the poem

*Partygate- the scandal of partying in Downing Street in the UK by ex-PM Boris Johnson while in office during Covid-19 restrictions

**The Child Q case in the UK - about a Black child who was strip-searched by the Police

THE ALMOST-PEARL IN THE MOON

A quiet sky,

Holding its breath,

For a new story, a new life.

Naked trees, each branch soaring high.

A hurt and an inoculation.

Pain laid bare.

Engulfing a half-formed hope

In the almost-pearl of the moon.

Hesitant, expectant.

The blanket of gathering darkness

Reigns in lurking ghosts,

Keeps warm a new dawn.

TAINTED AND DENTED, EXPECTING TO BE TREATED

They wheeled her in,

Naked, bloodied, raw entrails hanging.

Her private spaces violated by rusty rods,

And lustful men in a public bus.

The doctors said: "She brought it on herself."

The attendants viewed her askance,

Whispered behind her back: "Pull the tube!"

"Let us not waste a bed for immoral persons."

The nurses muttered: "She brought it on herself."

"Out with her boyfriend late at night."

"She deserves what she got!"

"That's it now, nobody will marry her."

"The tainted one, the dented one"

"Shameless" the manager barked,

Grudging her a ventilator, a pint of blood.

"We have got real patients waiting!"

The intern, fumbling to insert a venous line,
Saw the girl feebly grip her mother's hand.
"I want to live" and "Speak to the police."
She did; calmly in unflinching detail.

As the doctors pondered and bustled
With grim gazes and pursed lips.
Her mother saw, in their unsmiling faces,
The girl's life ebbing away.

But the will to survive coursing through her ravaged frame
Found a voice in the millions marching outside.
Burned in the candles in their cupped hands,
Nestled in the posy of flowers at her bedside.

Ministers conferred in huddled groups,
Flew her to a plush hospital in the hush of the night,
Where she lost the battle for life
In an alien land.

Yet her spirit lingered and lurked as she lay enshrouded,
Long after the bed was stripped and scrubbed,
The clothes were incinerated,
And the doctors had gone.

UNTIL WE ALL BREATHE FREE AGAIN

A dark night in the theatre of death,

Breaths keeping time to a soulless beeping.

Tears of grief flowing into iPads blue.

The walls bare, beseeching.

As I walk outside, guiltily thankful

For my icy breath leaching into the inky night;

Around me, autumn leaves drifting, rotting,

A mute marking of the fallen dead.

A tiny virus, mighty hubris

A callous culling of the old, and whose "sin is the colour of their skin."

Underlying health conditions,

Overlying contempt, discrimination.

A fight back

One mask, one test at a time.

Two metres, two doses of vaccines.

Standing afar, reaching out.

Holding close through the airwaves

For a slice of sun, a sliver of moon.

A tiny bud of spring,

Until we all breathe free again.

IT IS ALL IN THE MIND

He has a pain that doesn't go away.
"What is it, doctor?" he asks.
At the hospital, they shrug and mumble,
"It is difficult to say."

The malaise without a name
Has made him its home.
'It is all in your mind,' they say,
'Your body is fine.'

His body, with a mind of its own,
Hoards up its secrets,
Continues to baffle them
And consume him.

He wants them to understand,
To cross this chasm of not knowing.
He wants to bridge the gap.
Between his agony and their incomprehension.

He can see it in their eyes though,

Busy yet patient, firmly in control.

They are polite and well-meaning,

But they need to move on.

To the tumours they can cut,

To the hormones they can contain.

To the limbs that do their bidding,

To the fats that melt under their onslaught.

He is keeping them waiting,

Those patients who can help them reach targets.

Who will not question what they say,

Who will have good 'outcome measures.'

The time they spend on him;

They could take out a dozen appendices,

Do hundreds of scans.

Is it fair that he deprives so many of their care?

He wants to recover under their tree of knowledge

And be nourished with their sap of hope.

But in the set of their shoulders; the finality of their voice,

"There is nothing more we can do except refer you to mental health."

He thanks them, walks away.

The constant refrain keeping step with him,

"It is all in their mind,

"This fear without a name."

DARE TO DREAM

As the old year sputters

And gasps into its last night

Without a backward glance,

And the new year enters warily in,

As we follow the old well-worn rhythm

Mask, test, disinfect, jab,

And remember to breathe,

Do we dare to dream?

A year where dinghies deflated;

Egos inflated,

Refugees drowned,

And rogues fled.

A year where those who dared

To ask for a share of the world

That had been created

Out of their blood, sweat & tears;

Stretched their hands to the "first world"

To grasp a sliver of dignity for themselves

Ended in a coffin of cruel waves,

A shroud of cold indifference.

A nameless, watery grave

An Epitaph- "Beware all ye who enter here,"

The last rites intoned of Government stand-offs,

"Go back to where you came from."

A year where even more

Cold and unforgiving

Were the power games

Of people in warm homes.

Where the land empire may have shrunk

But spread its tentacles into icy waters instead.

To dream or not to dream

That's the question.

Do people who dare to dream

Have to be of a specific colour,

From a particular place

Or speak an elite language?

Do those who dare to hope!

For a better life

Have to perish

At fences, walls, borders and shores?

Let us not create another pandemic

Of bigotry and privilege.

A world of the dare-to-dreamers

And another of the dare-not-dreamers.

Let us greet and make a new year.

A new era where every dream starts

From a fragment of imagination and possibilities.

From dreams in repose to a wakeful repurposing.

LEST THEIR BEDS LIE EMPTY TONIGHT

Hark! A ball of fire.
A bullet or the sun?

Be still,
Stand straight,
Hands up.
Lest a bullet go astray,

In a hair's breadth, the blink of an eye.
Propelled by the hubris of uniform
And the colour of your skin.
Taser or gun or sometimes both.

A live youngster in an alley one minute,
In the next, a roadside corpse.
A shroud of crimson and cloud,
A dirge of birdsong.

Hug your boys tight,

Lest their beds lie empty tonight.

Rest tonight and then rise, rise

To continue the good fight.

A PLACE OF SAFETY

It was her fifth stop that night

In search of a place of safety.

The smell of stale food, fresh urine, old clothes,

And the rank odour of fear trailed her; glued to her skin.

She was too old for the children's ward,

Too young for the adults' unit.

Too risky for the children's home,

Too unwell for the police cell; too well for Casualty.

No beds in the borough, sorry.

Then back in the police van, long miles.

Driven through the heart of darkness,

In search of a place of safety.

It started after her seventeenth birthday,

When the demons from the past came again.

She screamed, swore, punched, kicked,

For the voices and images to go away.

They danced, relentless, in front of her

Till she was numb, exhausted.

The fight oozing out of her cuts red and thick.

Squeezing shut her veins, her face bloodless white.

The doctors, social worker, police officer

Warily stepped in, trespassing into her private hell.

"You are detained under the Mental Health Act."

"We will take you to a place of safety."

Numbers rent the air; words bounced off her headphones.

13 foster placements, 24/7 observations, date of birth.

"Challenging, abusive, aggressive, hostile,"

"Transition policy, serious untoward incident."

Onto a sterile, soulless room;

A nurse next to her bed, one in the corridor.

She prowled in the space like a caged tiger,

Finally took the tablets the nurse held out.

Welcome oblivion soon set in,

The journey halted but only briefly.

A respite before her search ended

For a place of safety.

A thought nagged at her; she pushed it away.

Was it in the ageless land of the dead where there was no fear or favour,

Where a place was always assured?

A place of safety.

WHEREFORE, STORMY SPRING?

What tune do you play, Spring?

The mournful wail of sirens

Or the hopeful notes of Frozen - "Let it go"?

The loud roar of male egos,

Or the quiet slumber of the innocent?

Here's how you show your myriad hues, Spring?

In the land of blue and yellow, hope leaching out into the cold.

Daylight bringing with it the stench of warfare.

Bodies crushed into permanent silence,

The colour of skin costing lives at borders.

Wherein lies beauty, Spring?

In the gently bowing grace of snowdrops,

Vying with the harsh forking glare of bombs?

The daffodils pushing proudly upright,

or in cruel hegemony digging its heels in?

What patterns the landscape, Spring?

The spikes on the Covid crown that continue to prick,

The chequered freezing & melting of a climatic seesaw.

Big hearts welcoming refugees "Come into our home,"

Or small minds keeping them out "Need more time, more documents."

But wait I also see in you Spring;

The sun rising earlier each day,

Lighting up dark spaces.

For every racist's rants;

Voices rising in unison, rescuing refugees.

Women with quiet grace preserving homes and heritage in friendly lands.

A man, erstwhile comedian now deadly serious;

Rallying his country with a war cry for freedom.

So arise stormy Spring, do what is right.

Wage, wage a war of love towards Summer bright.

FIRE IN OUR SOULS

They fanned a flame of cruelty and hate;

And spouted words of bigotry.

Hoping amity would be burned to cinders

And infighting would spread in the country.

They did not know

That words could be poison but the potion too.

We would temper the steel of our pens;

With the fire in our souls true.

Bearing the shield of courage and hope

Armed with the sword of resolve,

We will etch a map of peace;

And fill it with the hues of humanity and love.

THE FRAGMENTS OF A DAY

Blossom and barrenness;
Birdsong, dusk quiet.

The sun a fiery orange to a muted purple.
Winding roads, trees upright.

The silent breathing of those in repose
The gurgling breathlessness of those in the grip of the virus.

On my way home
Gathering the remnants of a day

A lungful of air, a fistful of hope.
I will not go gently into the night.

A SONG OF SILENCE

Between the anguished cries of the bereft
And the triumphant roar of the heedless,

Between a breath-squeezing hug
And a breathtaking virus,
Between a pyre being lit
And hope being extinguished,

Between the rippling of the river and the ebbing of the
tide,
Between the lowing of the cows
And the mewling of the lambs,
The cackling of the geese and the cawing of the gulls,

Between the splendour of the dawn
And the storminess of the clouds,
While the sun sets
And the moon glows,

In that heartbeat of time,

There's a stillness,

A silence which helps me listen

Deep within, and to those around me.

To my loved ones,

And to those unknown and unloved too,

A song unfurls in tiny whispers,

Trying to form a melody, weaving together

Harmonious notes of courage, honesty, and hope,

Rising above discordant notes of fear, uncertainty, and despair,

Which nudges me

To breathe life into something new.

Which helps me walk in my mind's lanes,

To forge a path towards gratitude and purpose,

To be me; all of me,

So I can help others be all of them.

AN INESCAPABLE RIGHTNESS OF BEING

The drumbeat of the motherland seeps into the bones,

Heightening senses and feeling,

The harsh tenor of the daily grind

Softened by the lilt of old melodies and new tongues.

The heart syncs to the rhythm of ageless sounds,

The cawing of crows;

The revving of auto-rickshaws,

The warning hiss before the whistle of the pressure cooker.

There is another identity; the colour of migration,

That I cannot now unknow,

That sometimes contrasts with my base foundation,

And makes me stare at my two-toned self in the mirror.

When I land; a brief misstep then a remembered gait takes over,

Retracing memory maps with the compass of belonging.

My voice does not falter while making itself heard,

Its timbre amplified by matching cadences.

My head feels lighter, au naturel,

It has shed the invisible cloak of foreignness,

My body does not apologise for taking up space,

Its presence has an inescapable rightness of being.

I ROOT FOR LOVE, ONE MORE TIME

The earth has discharged its latest quake;

The living and the dead entwined, freezing amongst the rubble.

Days later, a baby smiles tremulously, rescued from the ruins;

And I root for love, one more time.

The knife slices through yet another breast

When the young turn on the young in deadly battles.

Then I see the young fighting for their planet, their future,

And I root for love, one more time.

A young woman's fatal unveiling

Of her tresses turns them into a noose of death.

Women cut off their hair in solidarity and defiance,

And I root for love, one more time.

The colour of skin a harsh, discordant tone in the palette of justice;

Racism kills, and speaking up is a millstone round your neck.

A Black nurse bravely takes on the establishment and wins*,

And I root for love, one more time.

*This was a landmark case in the UK where a Black nurse won her case of racial discrimination against her employers

THE VOICE OF WOMAN

Flashing silver and gold,

Gathering strength as it flows,

Filling hollow crevices;

Reclaiming spaces, bridging divides.

Sometimes getting down on its haunches,

Before springing afresh,

Sometimes a rippling cadence,

Limned by the fiery sun.

Maintaining a quiet vigil,

Announcing its fearless presence,

Earth, water, air, fire,

The voice of woman.

NO WRONG DOOR

Knocked on the wrong door,

The doorway to death,

Pulled back from the brink,

To get up and catch a breath.

To have the right

To stand up and say,

There is no wrong door

And there is a right of way.

These tides of wrongness-

Being the wrong colour of skin,

Being in the wrong place,

Indeed where being is a sin.

Will not recede

With the moon or the sun,

The deadly wall of exclusion

Is shored up by society's collusion.

"Stop knocking", "You will die"

Have for too long been the street names,

With "All welcome here", "No wrong door",

We now need to rebuild; reclaim the lanes.

The gun of small-minded hatred

And the bullet of privilege,

Can only be neutralised

With the fire of love, tempered by courage.

LEST PRIDE HOLD SWAY ONCE AGAIN

The bomb of atomic might exploded,
Shattering the placid rhythm of the morn,
The choking engulfing cloud
Darkening the innocent sky.

Charred clothes melted onto unsuspecting backs,
Disembodied hands scattered about,
Their watches frozen in time welded into the pavement,
Blazing heads severed, bloodless hearts ripped from their chests.

Living ghosts with morphed faces
And burning trailing sheets of skin,
Blindly leaping into the river
Swollen with bodies & acid rain.

Power without love
And head without heart; people as pawns,
Helps till a soil ripe
For a nuclear snuffing of life.

The children of this hate

Are poised to turn either way,

Let the strength in humility beckon,

Lest pride hold sway once again.

From the mushroom cloud of death,

Spring blossoms can bloom,

The sky can shine blue once more,

And gently can the river flow.

REMNANTS OF THE SEASON

The sun bows with panache
On the season's stage;
Its summery bill of play as the lead actor
Draws to a close.
Its self-care schedule has begun
With daily lie-ins and early nights.

New transitions await
Between the acorn and the oak.
A chilly alliance
Between the wind and the trees,
A gentle melding
Of the earth and the leaves.

The autumn blushes molten
On the edge of debut;
Dressed in demure colours
And a bowed visage,
The hushed swishing of its dress
Made of the remnants of the season.

THE LONGEST JOURNEY

I remember rushing along in my white coat,

Past the long queues of the weary and the uncomplaining,

Patients who were desperately hoping to be seen that day,

So they would not have to spend their pennies on another bus journey.

Sleeping on the pavement so they could be first in line,

Touching my feet, grateful and overcome

Because I gave them ten minutes after a six-hour wait,

Barely glancing at them as I fired questions hurriedly.

They stared in silent incomprehension,

As I loudly rattled off Latin names

Of maladies and their medicines

In the packed open-plan clinic.

They filed out with bent heads,

Clutching the prescription like a protective armour,

Their eyes were knowing though,

With endurance, patience, and untold stories.

On the wards, they were herded like cattle,

Stripped of dignity along with their clothes,

Then gowned in suitable language, with a hat of risk assessments,

Accessorised with protocols and pathways.

The families had a self-respect all their own,

The old mother cleaning up after her son wordlessly,

Relatives round the bed

Skipping their meal to buy a syringe, a catheter for their loved one.

Flies buzzing overhead, the broken-down fan,

The threadbare sheet on the sagging cot with the musty, urine-soaked mattress,

The lunch trolley rattling on the tiled floor,

The runny lentils with an oil slick on top.

There is the patient, the cardiologist has checked his heart,

His joints manipulated by the rheumatologist,

His eyes gazed at by an ophthalmologist,

And his nerves tested by the neurologist.

He asks, "Who will look at me, the whole of me?"
"Oh wait there isn't a protocol for that,"
"Which part of the body does that come under?"
"I will talk to my manager."

The patient, still waiting,
"All I want, all I ask
Is to see me life-size
Not bust size, not profile, not passport size."

"Not to fit me into a protocol
But a protocol to fit me,
With space for my hopes and fears,
My joys and tears."

He ignores a routine follow-up letter.
"Patient did not attend," they say.
I say the doctor did not attend,
Not with their heart and mind.

The computer did,
And so did a lot of forms.
Tests and treatments tagged along,
The patient is now duly discharged.

I have come a long way

From one country to another,

But there is a road less travelled,

A path poorly illuminated.

They are in front of each other, about to set off,

The doctor and the patient.

The route toward the art of healing

Is the longest journey of all.

THE FINAL TOUCH

The dreaded shrill of the telephone
Tore through the silence of the night,
Bringing with it a message
Of the beginning of the end.

Far away across land and sea,
On the soulless steel of a hospital bed,
Mum lay gasping for breath,
Playing hide and seek with death.

"Come straightaway,"
My dad's voice wobbled.
"Mum is waiting for you,"
The unspoken "So we can face this together."

The plane crested the clouds and turned
Towards the land of my birth.
My heart plumbed the depths of despair,
My voice rose in prayer.

Would she recognise me?

Would she call me by her special name for me?

The rays of hope shortened,

As the spectre of death grew longer.

Mum was dying, in unbearable pain.

The adult me realised this and grieved.

But the selfish, plaintive child in me

Wailed and railed at the abandonment.

The plane cruised dizzyingly high,

Aeons passed; it was agonisingly slow

From the airport to the hospital.

The moment I entered, I wrestled with the inevitable.

As I crossed the threshold towards her bed,

The world turned upside down.

Mum lay frail and small, in a foetal curl.

I bent over, crooned to her, held water to her lips.

Was a miracle possible- could I be her life-giving parent?

Mum moved, looked me in the eye, called my name.

She then quietly turned her back on life,

And embraced death with a sigh.

Her face serene,

Far away from pain and strife.

My daughter softly called out "Granny,"

And brought new life gently back into the room.

www.ingramcontent.com/pod-product-compliance
Lightning Source LLC
Chambersburg PA
CBHW021142130726
47988CB00003B/1422